Endurance

I am an Overcomer

Tianna Williams

Paperback   ISBN: 978-1-960853-82-0

Liberation's Publishing House LLC
Columbus - Mississippi

Acknowledgements

"And they overcame him by the blood of the Lamb, and by the word of their testimony." Revelation 12:11KJV

First and foremost, I give all honor and glory to the Most High God. Without His grace and mercy, I truly don't know where I would be. It is only because of Him that I am alive, thriving, and able to share this part of my journey.

To my mother, Tanya Williams, and my father, Andre Pratt—thank you. Without you, I wouldn't be here. To my brothers, Rashad Williams and Judan Pratt, and to my aunt, Annette Coleman—you've been more than family; you've been a steady source of love, support, and care, especially when you didn't have to be. I'm grateful beyond words.

To all of my godparents—from those who've known me since birth to those who've joined my life as I've grown—thank you for your presence and influence. And to my extended family and friends who have stood by me through thick and thin—your loyalty and love mean the world to me.

To *Kingdom Driven*, under the leadership of Elder Darius Brown along with his wife Prophetess Santana Brown, along with Deacon Frankie Crump and his wife Elder Jamelia Crump, and Prophetess Kelcey Bean—thank you for challenging me daily to grow in Christ. Your accountability, encouragement, and unwavering faith have helped mold me into who I am today. I am forever grateful for this divine connection.

A special thank you to Pastor Delorise Parks and Apostle Shelia Howell—your guidance, prayers, wisdom, and consistent encouragement have been instrumental in shaping my walk and leadership. I am blessed to have you both in my life.

While I may not have named everyone, please know that every act of kindness, every word of encouragement, and every prayer offered has not gone unnoticed. You each play a special role in my story, and I carry you in my heart with deep appreciation.

To Prophetess Kelcey Bean—thank you for being the push I needed to see this book through to completion. Your persistence, love, and support made all the difference. I am honored to call you my friend.

And finally, to Prophetess Deona Benson—thank you for your obedience to the voice of God and for confirming the call over my life to write this book. Your words ignited something in me, and I will always be grateful for your faithfulness.

With all my love, Tianna

Table of Contents

Introduction

Have you ever asked God, "Why me?"

Most of us have. I know I definitely have—many times. In life, we all face trials and tribulations that leave us questioning, "Why me? What did I do so wrong to deserve this?"

Almost instinctively, our minds jump to what we've been taught all our lives: *You reap what you sow.* Suddenly, every mistake, every poor decision, every failure flashes through our thoughts. We begin to replay all the things we've done that we believe may have displeased God, desperately trying to connect the dots between our actions and the suffering we're experiencing.

We wrestle with painful questions deep within ourselves: *I know I'm not perfect, but did I really deserve to be molested at the age of ten? What sin was so great that my innocent child was born battling cancer? Yes, I've been disobedient. Yes, I've made poor choices. But did I really deserve to suffer from kidney failure at just twelve years old?*

I am guilty of questioning God—especially during moments of deep pain and overwhelming struggle. But the truth is, life itself is a series of trials and tribulations. **No one is exempt.** It doesn't matter your race, your religious beliefs, your political views, or your financial status—life will bring challenges to us all. Pain, loss, and hardship are part of the human experience.

Yet, there is good news. **You can overcome.** You can endure. You are not alone.

Jesus said in John 16:33 (KJV), *"These things I have spoken unto you, that in me ye might have peace. In the world ye shall have tribulation: but be of good cheer; I have overcome the world."*

As you continue reading this book, my prayer is that it encourages you to live with hope and confidence, knowing that no matter what you are facing right now—you can overcome. I pray it stirs your faith to new heights and reminds you that if God brought me through my darkest seasons, **He can surely do the same for you.**

You are not forgotten. You are not alone. Victory is within your reach.

Chapter 1 Why Me?

Tuesday, February 13th, 2001 — a day forever etched in my memory. I was riding home on the school bus when, without warning, my body went numb. My vision blurred, and tears streamed down my face. My mouth was so dry I could barely speak, let alone move. I truly believed I was having a stroke—I thought I was going to die.

That was the moment everything changed.

I somehow managed to get off the bus, forcing myself to walk toward a neighbor's house to get help. I didn't make it. I fainted before I could even knock on the door. The next thing I remember was waking up to a cold rag being placed on my forehead as I was rushed to the North Mississippi Medical Clinic.

It's true what they say—life can change in an instant. Mine did, in the blink of an eye.

I'll never forget the moment the doctor walked in and gave us the diagnosis: **complete renal failure in both kidneys.** I was only 12 years old. I was stunned. Confused. Terrified.

Questions flooded my mind faster than I could form them: *What does this mean? How could this happen to me? Will I ever be normal again? What about school? What about basketball?*

I was just a child—how could I possibly make sense of any of it?

Tears kept falling as the weight of the unknown settled in. I looked over at my mother, trying so hard to be strong, holding back her emotions for my sake. My grandmother and aunt were there, too—all of us overwhelmed, all of us searching for answers that even the doctors didn't have.

The next step: transfer to North Mississippi Medical Center.

And with that, my journey truly began.

Have you ever been in a place in your life where everything was going well and all of a sudden everything changed?

Think about this moment. What happened? How did it make you feel?

_____
_____
_____
_____
_____
_____
_____
_____
_____
_____

Immediately, the doctors began sticking my arm with needles to draw blood, inserting IVs to pump calcium and other medications into my body. It was all happening so fast. I couldn't help but ask, *Why me?*

My family didn't have the answers I was looking for—no explanations to ease my confusion or pain—but what they gave me instead was faith. And the truth is, their faith-filled response was the best answer they could have given.

I thank God my grandmother raised me in church, because in that moment, I had to lean on everything I had been taught. Without that spiritual foundation, I would have been completely lost. I may not have understood the "why," but I dared not question the power of faith I had come to know.

And honestly, that was better than any answer.

Parents, it's very important to take your child to church and read the Bible to them at a young age. You may not think that they're listening, but they are. Proverbs 22:6 says train up a child in the way he should go, and when he is old he will not depart from it. KJV

As I was spending my Valentine's Day in the hospital, the doctors continued running blood tests, X-rays, and biopsies, searching for answers about what caused my kidney failure—but they found none. No explanation. No root cause. I was eventually transferred to Le Bonheur Children's Hospital, where I could receive more specialized care.

I can't even begin to describe the dramatic changes my body went through. Yet through it all, I found the truth in scripture—when Jesus told Paul, *"My grace is sufficient for thee, for my strength is made perfect in weakness"* (2 Corinthians 12:9). I didn't know how strong I was until I had no choice but to be strong.

My grandmother and aunt always reminded me, *"God will never put more on you than you can bear."* And the truth is, if our Heavenly Father didn't believe we could handle "it"—whatever your *it* may be—He wouldn't have allowed it to come into our lives.

If you're feeling overwhelmed—by sickness, depression, financial struggles, grief, loneliness, divorce, or anything else—I have one word for you: **fight.**

Don't give up. Fight your way through. You *can* and *will* make it.

To fight means to keep moving forward, even when everything inside you wants to quit. Wake up and declare:
"I am healed."

"I am a winner."

"I will not lose this battle."

Show up. Go to school, go to work, go to church—even when you don't feel like it. Don't let your emotions control your purpose. Smile even when it hurts. Let your pain fuel your determination, not your defeat.

I'm not sharing something I haven't lived through. Even at the age of 12 and 13, I had to remind myself to fight daily. I learned to fight through **prayer and praise**, and eventually, those two things built my faith. I prayed because I knew God was my supreme ruler. And over time, my prayers birthed my praise.

No matter how hopeless your situation may seem, **God can do anything.** He brings dead things back to life. *"With God, all things are possible"* (Mark 10:27). I'm a living witness that when you pray and praise, God will show up and move on your behalf.

On **August 1st, 2002**, while in Toledo, Ohio, we received a phone call from Le Bonheur. They said they had a kidney and were trying to decide who would receive it. My family prayed. The saints prayed. And I prayed.

Later, they called back and said the words I'll never forget: **"Come to Memphis. The kidney is yours."**

What a mighty God we serve!

I received **victory over dialysis** and **victory over kidney failure**. When I was first diagnosed, my great-grandmother prophesied that God had shown her I would receive a new kidney. It didn't happen overnight, but we must learn to stand firm on the promises of God. *"Though it linger, wait for it; it will certainly come and will not delay"* (Habakkuk 2:3).

Whatever you're going through—**fight.** Fight with the Word. Fight in your secret place. Fight through prayer, faith, fasting, and **never forget to fight with praise.**

"God inhabits the praises of His people" (Psalm 22:3).

For every problem, there is a solution. And for every solution, another opportunity for God to get the glory.

So instead of asking, *"Why me?"*
I now ask, *"Why not me?"*
Why not let God get the glory out of my life?

Because He brought me through, I can now help others know: **you can overcome too.**

"They overcame him by the blood of the Lamb and by the word of their testimony" (Revelation 12:11).

I am an overcomer... And so are you.

Tianna Williams 9

Chapter 2 God's Love

Here that loveth not knoweth not God, for God is love.

1 John 4:8.

Nine weeks into the school year, it was time for progress reports. Everyone was buzzing—some excited to share their grades, others not so much. I had always been an A and B student, so I usually felt confident. But this time, I was nervous.

When I opened my report, my heart sank.

There it was—a big, bold **F** staring back at me.

Now, my grandmother was understanding as long as she knew I was doing my best. But an **F**? That was something she simply would not accept.

As soon as I got home, I rushed to my bedroom. I sat on the floor, took a pen, and changed the grade from an F to a B. Then I did what I knew how to do—I prayed.

"Lord," I whispered, "You can let anything happen to me… just please don't let my grandmother find out about this grade."

And, truth be told, she never did.

But not long after that moment, something much bigger happened.

I found out I had **kidney failure.**

Have you ever done something that you knew was wrong, but you did it anyway and then prayed that you wouldn't get caught?

It took me a while to tell anyone, but the truth is—deep down inside, I believed I was the cause of my own sickness.

I was raised in the church. I knew right from wrong, and I knew about sin and its consequences. Changing my grade felt like a lie, and I couldn't shake the guilt. I remembered the words from *Psalm 101:7*: *"He who practices deceit shall not dwell within my house; he who tells lies shall not continue in my presence."*

I feared the judgment of God, but I didn't yet understand the **depth** of His love.

I knew John 3:16—*"For God so loved the world that He gave His only begotten Son..."* I understood that Jesus' sacrifice proved God's love, but I didn't grasp that His love also means **new mercy** every single day. As it says in *Lamentations 3:22-23*: *"It is because of the Lord's mercies that we are not consumed... they are new every morning."*

For a long time, I lived on pins and needles—trapped in fear and guilt—not because God didn't love me, but because I didn't fully **understand** His love.

Let me be clear: I'm not promoting sin. Jesus is against sin. The Bible tells us in *Romans 6:23*, *"The wages of sin is death."* And in *John 14:15*, Jesus says, *"If you love Me, keep My commandments."* So yes, we should strive to live a life that pleases God.

But on this journey of faith, we're still in these fleshly bodies—and we will fall short. That's why *1 John 2:1-2* is so powerful: *"My little children, I write this to you so that you may not sin. But if anyone does sin, we have an Advocate with the Father—Jesus Christ, the Righteous One. He is the atoning sacrifice for our sins—and not only for ours but also for the sins of the whole world."*

That was the part I had to grow into.

I had to mature in Christ to understand that my kidney failure wasn't a punishment for changing my grade. Sure, if my grandmother or teacher had found out, there would have been consequences—but not divine condemnation.

Yes, some consequences are directly related to our choices. But not every trial is the result of sin. Sometimes, God allows us to walk through hardship so **He** can be glorified through our lives.

That's the point I want to make.

My kidney failure—and the miracle of my transplant—weren't about punishment. They were about **purpose**. They were part of God's plan to get glory out of my life.

As born-again believers, we should expect trials and tribulations. They test our faith and strengthen our relationship with God. Trials are not the same as consequences. While consequences are the natural results of actions, trials can be divine opportunities for growth and testimony.

God is not a tyrant waiting to punish you for every mistake. He is a **loving Father**, full of grace and mercy. He knows our hearts. He knows when we are truly sorry—and He also knows when we're just trying to avoid the outcome.

The truth is, **God doesn't hurt us—we hurt ourselves.** And even then, His love still surrounds us.

"My son, do not despise the chastening of the Lord, nor be weary of His correction" (Proverbs 3:11).

Yes, we should fear God—but not out of terror. We fear Him in reverence, because of who He is: our Father, our protector, our provider, our redeemer.

There's a difference between consequences for sin and adversity for His glory. And now I understand that **He allowed my trial not to destroy me, but to display His power through me.**

God loves you. And He's not finished with your story.

For whom the Lord loveth, He corrected, even as a father, the Son in whom He delighteth. Proverbs 3:11-12

As many as I love, I rebuke, and our chasten be zealous therefore, and repent. Revelations 3:14.

There is No Fear in love, but perfect. Perfect love cast out fear, because fear hath torment. He that feareth is not made perfect in love. First John 4:18.

For God so loved the world that he gave His only begotten Son, that whosoever believeth in him should not perish, but have everlasting life. John 3:16.

And we have known and believed the love that God has for us. God is love, and he that dwelleth in love dwelleth in God, and God in him. First, John 4:16.

Allow God to teach you how to love like "him"!

Meditation Questions:

1. **Have I ever tried to "fix" a mistake in secret rather than face the truth?**
    - What motivated that decision—fear, shame, pride?
    - How did it affect my relationship with God?
2. **Do I associate hardship or illness with punishment?**
    - Can I identify any trials in my life that actually revealed God's presence or purpose?
3. **What is my current understanding of God's love?**
    - Do I view Him more as a harsh judge or a compassionate Father?
    - How can I grow in embracing His "new mercies every morning" (Lamentations 3:23)?

4. **Have I ever felt like I was beyond forgiveness?**
   - What Scriptures or experiences help me believe that Jesus is my advocate, even when I fall short (1 John 2:1-2)?

5. **What's the difference between a consequence of sin and a God-ordained trial in my life?**
   - How can I discern the difference and respond accordingly?

6. **Am I walking in reverent fear of the Lord—or paralyzing fear of judgment?**
   - What does "perfect love casts out fear" (1 John 4:18) mean in my daily walk?

7. **What is one past failure I need to surrender to God—not as a curse, but as part of His plan for purpose and glory?**

8. **Do I believe that God delights in me—even when I've messed up?**
   - How can I rest in the truth of Proverbs 3:12: *"For whom the Lord loves He corrects..."*?

Chapter 3 God's Plan vs Man's Plan

Standing on the sidelines, watching my older cousins play basketball, brought me so much joy. I was really young at the time, so playing with them wasn't an option—but the moment they finished, I would run to the ball and try to imitate every move I had just seen. It was as if basketball was woven into my DNA—a natural gift from God.

It wasn't something I had to work hard at; it simply flowed. Basketball became an escape, a release. No matter what I was going through, I left it all on the court. I dreamed of playing in the WNBA—and I meant it. At one point, I believed basketball was my future—the one thing I could do to make money and truly enjoy doing it.

I used to watch my favorite players and mimic their every move with my brother. I would tell him, "I'm going to be just like them." In high school, I made a habit of heading straight to the gym after lunch. Those moments were pure joy—laughing, playing, bonding with my friends.

But I'll never forget what happened one day in 2006.

As I was walking from the cafeteria to the gym, something different happened. The Holy Spirit visited me. I began to feel His presence so deeply that tears started flowing. It was as if I was walking on clouds. I felt weightless, like I wasn't even in my own body. In that sacred moment, I heard the voice of God say, **"Preach My Word."**

God was letting me know I had been chosen to do a great work for Him.

I still can't fully explain what I felt or how I even made it to the gym that day—but what I do know is that my life changed forever. Everything I had planned no longer seemed to align with what God was saying. But that's not just my story—it's many people's story. We all make plans, but God often redirects them.

Through my experience, I've learned how important it is to live in obedience to God. So often we want to be in His will, but on **our** terms. That's one of the most dangerous positions to take. When we operate that way, we're essentially saying, *"God, I hear You, but I'm still going to do it my way."* But we must trust God with every area of our life. He desires complete surrender. Even when we don't understand His plan, **He knows what's best for us.**

In my heart, I was willing to lay down every dream—even basketball—to follow God's voice. Though I still enjoy playing from time to time, pursuing it as a career was no longer an option. I realized I couldn't give God 100% and still chase my personal dreams with the same intensity.

As Prophetess Deanna Benson once said: *"When you give your life to God, you've died."*

In other words, my life was no longer just about me. It was about Him—His will, His purpose, His Kingdom.

I bring this up to stress the importance of living **unselfishly**. Selfishness can easily get in the way of our relationship with God. Many people struggle with letting go of control, but the truth is— **God is a God who interrupts.** And we must allow Him to do so. He knows what He's doing. Because of my love for God, it didn't take long for me to surrender to the call. Preaching wasn't something I had ever desired, but obedience mattered more to me.

I gave my life to the Lord at the age of 12. I knew even then that I wanted to live for Him, though I didn't fully understand what came with that commitment. As I grew older, I began to understand more deeply that it wasn't about me—it was about building God's Kingdom.

I'm not saying God won't bless your dreams—He absolutely can. The Bible says, *"Delight yourself in the Lord, and He will give you the desires of your heart"* (Psalm 37:4). But being completely sold out to Him sometimes means letting go of what we thought life would be, so He can give us something greater.

His will, not mine—that's what I continue to remind myself of daily.

We must remember: **God is real, and there is life after death.** The way we live now determines where we'll spend eternity. If we fail to repent and give God our heart, hell will be our destination. But if we surrender, repent, and give our lives completely to Him, **heaven will be our eternal home**.

Let God have complete control. You'll never regret surrendering to His will.

Proverbs 16:9, a man's heart deviseth his way; but the Lord directeth his steps. (KJV)

Roman 8:28, "And we know that all things work together for the good t them that love God, to them who are called according to his purpose. (KJV)

Biblica Examples'

- Paul persecutor to an Apostle.
- David, sheep keeper to a king.
- Gideon, poor man to the judge over Israel.

Ordinary men that most would look down on became great leaders. Their occupation wasn't what they had and planned. However, it was God's plan.

- Can you relate?
- Has God ever changed your plans?
- How did you respond?
- Are you living outside the will of God?

I was raised by my great-grandmother—a strong woman who had six children of her own and helped raise several grandchildren, including me. When she passed away, only a few of us were named in her will. I just so happened to be one of them.

Because I was in her will, I inherited many things. And oh, how thankful I was! I gained so much—not just materially, but emotionally. I felt seen, chosen, and valued.

But as I've grown in my spiritual walk, I've come to understand something even greater: **the most important will to be in is the will of God.**

- Are you in *His* will?
- Are you obeying His instructions?
- Have you overcome selfishness?

Selfishness is defined as *being excessively or exclusively concerned with one's own advantage, pleasure, or welfare— regardless of others* (*Wikipedia*). And let's be honest: it's a struggle we all face. But selfishness is one of the greatest hindrances to walking fully in God's will.

I pray that this chapter helps you recognize just how important it is to live in obedience to God—not just in some areas, but in **every** area of your life. The Bible teaches us in *Luke 9:23* that we must first **deny ourselves**, take up our cross daily, and follow Him.

God's plans are always better than ours.

There is **freedom**, **joy**, and **peace** when we surrender and walk in obedience. No, it won't always be easy. Obedience may cost you comfort, popularity, or even your own desires—but I promise you this: **it will be worth it.**

So I ask you again… are you in His will?

Because there's no inheritance greater than what you gain by living a life fully surrendered to God.

Chapter 4 Fighting with the Enemy

One day, while sitting in the kitchen at the table with my grandmother and aunt, we received a phone call that shook our world—there had been a sudden death in the family. The moment I heard the news, my body went into shock. My breathing became shallow, my vision blurred, my tongue went numb, and the side of my face started to tingle. I thought I was having a stroke. All I could envision was myself collapsing to the floor.

It was the second time in my life that my body had entered such a traumatic state. But this time, it wasn't kidney failure—it was the beginning of **anxiety**. So what is anxiety? It's a feeling of worry, nervousness, or unease, typically about an imminent event or something with an uncertain outcome.

You might say, *"Everyone deals with anxiety sometimes—what's the big deal?"*

But I beg to differ.

This wasn't occasional nervousness. This was a battle. **Living in fear had become part of my identity.**

- Have you ever faced anxiety?

- If so, how did you respond?
- Have you ever explored the root cause of your anxiety?

Because every issue has a root.

For me, it started young. I was raised in the church and taught to fear God. *Psalm 112:1* says, *"Blessed is the man that feareth the Lord."* That fear kept me out of trouble as a child. Though I wasn't perfect, that reverence helped guide many of my decisions. And for that, I'm grateful.

But I misunderstood what it meant to **fear God**.

I feared Him so much that I was afraid to truly talk to Him, to see Him as my Father. Yes, I prayed—but I lacked that deep, intimate relationship He desires from His children. My fear became so consuming that it didn't just affect my spiritual life—it began to take over my natural life, too.

Can you imagine living a holy life but walking on eggshells every day—saved, but not truly free?

It's not supposed to be like that.

It's like living with a father you desperately want to please, yet you're too afraid to sit and talk with him, to laugh with him, or simply be near him. That's not how God wants our relationship with Him to be. He is **loving**, **gentle**, and **approachable**.

Jesus said in *Matthew 11:28, "Come unto me, all ye that labor and are heavy laden, and I will give you rest."*

But how can you go to someone you're afraid to speak to? You can't.

That lack of understanding was the root of my anxiety. It would hit without warning and cripple me. I couldn't go anywhere alone. Eventually, a doctor prescribed **Xanax** to calm my body and help me sleep. I battled with this for about seven years.

But the Bible says in *2 Timothy 1:7, "For God has not given us the spirit of fear, but of power, and of love, and of a sound mind."*

Anxiety isn't just a disorder—it's a spirit, and it's not from God. Ask yourself: **Am I giving the enemy access to my life?**

It started with a persistent headache I couldn't shake. Tylenol didn't help. The rest didn't help. It got so bad that I didn't want to be home alone, so I went to my cousin's house nearby. That night I tossed and turned; the pain unbearable. The next morning, I went to work, trying to push through—but after two hours, my vision blurred again. I left and went back to my cousin's house hoping sleep would bring relief.

It didn't.

My body felt like it was shutting down. Swallowing became difficult. I was fading. Then, suddenly, I experienced something terrifying: **a spiritual attack**.

I was kidnapped—spiritually—by the enemy. He grabbed me and threw me onto the back of a pickup truck. I screamed at the top of my lungs trying to get away. The enemy had a hold on me so strong, it felt impossible to break free. He appeared as a Caucasian man with white and gray spiked hair. His grip was fierce, and his mission was clear—he was trying to **take me to hell**.

But every time he put me down, I found enough strength to get back up. He kept attacking, trying to weaken me so I couldn't fight back. But I refused to give in. I knew this was a spiritual battle for my soul. And though the enemy was strong, **God's power was stronger**.

I share this story to let you know: the devil is real. The spirit of fear tried to kill me—and it would have—**if God hadn't stepped in.** The only reason I'm alive is because **Satan did not have permission** to take my life.

"See now that I, even I, am he, and there is no god beside me: I kill, and I make alive..." (Deuteronomy 32:39, KJV).

This, you see, not only did I have anxiety that could have killed me, I also lost my mind. One may call it a nervous breakdown. In my mind I was having this experience with Satan, but realistically so. I was fighting with my family members and friends and my mind. It was the Caucasian man, but in real life it was people dear to me. To calm me down, the doctors had to highly sedate me, which caused me to have to go on a ventilator. I woke up in the ICU. Three days later I had a tube down my throat so I couldn't talk. Still slightly sedated so I was unable to see clearly. As I was waking up I heard the voice of God say grace saves you. It wasn't how many times I had preached. Drew people to Christ or how good of a Christian I thought I was. It was nothing but the grace of God that kept me alive. Thank God for grace and mercy.

Have you ever been in a situation that could have killed you but Grace intervened?

While I was in the hospital, many people came by to pray for me. I remember one visit in particular—my good friend, Bishop Calvin Darden. He came in quoting scriptures, declaring the Word of God over me, and boldly commanding the spirit of anxiety to leave my body and never return.

Lying there in that hospital bed, something shifted. It was in that moment that **God delivered me**.

Bishop Darden also gave me scriptures to speak over myself every day. I began building my faith and learning to speak life over my situation. Through that experience, I discovered the importance of **having God on your side**, knowing the scriptures, and recognizing the **power in God's Word**.

After I was released from the hospital, the doctors—and even some friends—encouraged me to see a psychologist. But I felt led to do something different. I scheduled an appointment with a **spiritual counselor** instead. My appointment was set for a Monday morning, just a few hours before work.

I'll never forget that day.

I had overslept and was running late. When I got to work, I stood outside with a yellow sticky note in my hand, preparing to call the counselor. Then, all of a sudden, the paper flew from my hand. I looked everywhere—but it was gone. The wind had taken it, but I hadn't even seen it blow away.

It felt like God Himself had snatched the paper from me. And in that exact moment, I heard Him speak clearly: **"Trust Me."** Without hesitation, I said, **"Yes, Lord."** From that point on, God began giving me specific instructions—and I followed them. That day, I made a choice: I would **fully trust** the God I serve in **every area** of my life. I'm happy to say that since then, I haven't had to take **Xanax** or **Vistaril**. In **2016**, I was completely **delivered from anxiety**.

And I have good news for you:

You can be delivered, too.

When you truly **surrender your life to God**, you give Him access to your mind, body, and soul. And anything in your life that is out of alignment has to **submit to His Word**.

- Anxiety is not from Jesus.
- Fear is not from Jesus.
- It is not God's will for you to live in fear when you were created to live in **freedom**.

Why hold on to anxiety—or anything else that's not from God—when **you can be free**?

The Bible says in *John 10:10*, *"The thief comes only to steal, kill, and destroy…"* That means anything you battle with that pulls you away from God's peace, joy, or purpose is a fight with the enemy. Maybe your battle isn't anxiety. Maybe it's **anger**, **lust**, **depression**, **shame**, or **doubt**. **Whatever it is**, if it hinders your ability to trust and obey God, it's a battle against Satan's tactics. You may not see the enemy face to face, but every time something causes you to act outside the will of God, you are in a **spiritual fight**.

Galatians 5:17 says, *"For the flesh lusteth against the Spirit, and the Spirit against the flesh: and these are contrary the one to the other: so that ye cannot do the things that ye would."*

Our flesh is constantly at war with the Spirit of God—but **victory is possible** through surrender and obedience.

I'm living proof that **God delivers**.
I am alive and in my right mind because of His **grace and mercy**.
Because of **prayer** and **faith**, I can boldly say:
With the help of Jesus, I have overcome anxiety.

My prayer for you is this:
Don't allow life to overtake you. Yes, things happen. Life changes. Loved ones pass. But don't let your pain turn into fear. Whatever your struggle is—**fight your way through.** Don't let it consume you. Stand in God's power and speak over your life. The only way to have power **over your issue** is through the **power of the Holy Ghost**. The enemy doesn't want you to have that power—because he wants to control you. But **with God, the enemy is powerless**.

Let that truth set you free.

Only **God** holds the power of life and death.

If you're battling anxiety or fear, know this: **God wants to set you free.** His perfect love casts out fear. He longs for a relationship with you—not based on fear, but built on love, trust, and truth.

You don't have to live on edge.
You don't have to be paralyzed by fear.
You don't have to surrender to anxiety.

Surrender to God.

Let Him take control.

He's not trying to scare you—He's trying to **save you**.

And if He can rescue me, He can rescue you too.

Chapter 5 Life with Jesus

For God so loved the world that he gave his only begotten son, that whosoever believeth in him should not perish, but have everlasting life. John 316.

Where would I be if it weren't for the love of God?

Most people love based on conditions—who you are, what you have, what you can offer. But God? He loves us simply because of **who we are**—His creation, made in **His image**.

He doesn't love you based on your family name, the color of your skin, where you come from, or how much money you have. His love is **unconditional** and **unchanging**. And I share this because my life **didn't begin to change** until I truly understood **the love of God**.

To know that no matter how broken or messed up someone is, **God is still there**, listening, waiting for us to love Him back—**that** is a powerful realization.

"If you love Me, keep My commandments." – **John 14:15**

But we must also understand this: we can't keep His commandments without **His Spirit** living inside of us.

"For the law of the Spirit of life in Christ Jesus has made me free from the law of sin and death." – **Romans 8:2**

Many people have **experienced** God. But I want to challenge you—**is experience enough?**

An experience is simply a moment—an event that may stir emotion, provide insight, or alter your perspective. It might make you cry, dance, or shout. But most of the time, it doesn't require much from you.

An **encounter** with God, however, requires something more. An encounter means both parties are involved. It demands response. It transforms. It causes change.

Growing up in church, I often felt God's presence. I witnessed His power. The atmosphere would shift, and His Spirit would move. Those moments were beautiful—and they assured me that God is real.

But when life got hard, **experiences weren't enough**.
I needed something deeper.

It wasn't until I decided to stop going back and forth—asking for forgiveness one day and returning to the same struggle the next—that I truly met Christ **face to face**.

I didn't just ask Him to forgive me.

I asked Him to **fill me**.

To fill me with the **Holy Spirit**, the power that helps us **resist the enemy**, **walk in order**, **stay clean**, and be made spiritually acceptable before God.

My **encounter** left me thirsty—not just for an emotional high, but for the **Word of God**. It ignited a hunger to know Him, please Him, and obey Him. The more I encountered the Holy Ghost, the more I desired a relationship. And the more life threw at me, the stronger that relationship became.

As I've shared in previous chapters, I've been through much:

Not knowing my father.

Battling anxiety.

Toxic relationships.

Loss.

Financial hardship.

Mental and spiritual attacks.

And yet—I'm still standing.

Why? Because of Jesus.

When people ask me how I made it through, my answer is always the   same:

Jesus.

That's why I stress this: it's not enough to have an experience. You need an **encounter**—a **face-to-face moment** with Christ that says:

"Lord, I'm not just here for what You can do for me. I'm here because I want to live for You. I want to be in Your will. I want my soul to be saved."

Living with Christ on the inside brings **everlasting life**. Without Him, all that's left is spiritual death.

"For the wages of sin is death, but the gift of God is eternal life through Christ Jesus our Lord." – **Romans 6:23**

So ask yourself:

- Are you still just **experiencing** Christ—or have you truly **encountered** Him?
- Have you fully **given Him your life**?
- Are you **living** or **dying** spiritually?

To please God means to **walk in obedience**.
And don't forget—there are only **two final destinations**: heaven or hell.

When you receive Christ and live according to His purpose, you walk in **freedom**. But if you reject His truth, you walk in **bondage**— a symbol of sin and death. That means **Satan becomes your master**.

Yes, life gets hard. But with Christ, there is **always hope**. He is the God who **rescues**, and the God who **never lies**.

"I will never leave you, nor forsake you." – **Hebrews 13:5**

That's His promise.
And I am a living witness that He keeps every single one.

Chapter 6 No Test No Testimony

From sickness to disability to insecurity to anxiety, financial Issues—being engaged, losing my mind, not knowing how to love, depression, being misunderstood, and dealing with unforgiveness. There was no way I would have been able to completely overcome without Jesus. Your situation may look better, but better is not best. Overcoming—the victorious answer to my life—seems simple yet powerful, with no questioning or doubt. The answer to all of my life's obstacles is Jesus.

We must understand that Satan knows our weak spots. And although one may have overcome, it doesn't mean Satan won't try to attack again. That's the importance of living in Jesus—knowing that He is fighting for us.

Exodus 14:14 (KJV): "The Lord shall fight for you, and ye shall hold your peace."

The Bible says in:

Romans 8:37 (KJV): "Nay, in all these things we are more than conquerors through him that loved us."

To conquer is to be victorious over an adversary. To be *more than a conqueror* means we not only achieve victory, but we are overwhelmingly victorious. Satan is our adversary, and his task is to kill, steal, and destroy by any means necessary.

To be victorious, you have to be on the winning side. **Whose side are you on?**

There are only two sides to be on: Jesus or Satan. Your lifestyle determines whose side you're on. Take this time to evaluate yourself:

- Have you given your heart to God?
- Have you put your belief into action?
- Do you obey His commandments?
- Do you die to yourself daily?

To be on the winning side means you're on the Lord's side. Sometimes, you may not feel like you're on the winning side—or look like it—but you must keep the faith, refer back to the Word of God, and allow it to encourage you.

Psalm 34:19 (KJV): "Many are the afflictions of the righteous: but the Lord delivereth him out of them all."

Matthew 6:26 (KJV): "Behold the fowls of the air: for they sow not, neither do they reap nor gather into barns; yet your heavenly Father feedeth them. Are ye not much better than they?"

3 John 1:2 (KJV): "Beloved, I wish above all things that thou mayest prosper and be in health, even as thy soul prospereth."

No matter how your situation may look right now, your relationship with Jesus should never die. You must learn to have an intimate relationship with God. Through the good times and the bad times, your love for Him should never waver.

Several times in my life, I could have given it all up—but because I had invested too much in my relationship with Jesus, I refused to let it all go to waste. I encourage you to strengthen your relationship with Christ by fasting, praying, reading your Word, and being obedient. Although I've overcome a lot, my relationship, faith, and past issues make my current situation a little easier. God knows you—but have you gotten to know Him? Give God all of you because He deserves it.

It's kind of like sports. If you want to win the championship, you must give it your all. Most athletes will tell you how they had to overcome many obstacles. In order to be successful, it's almost the same—except on the spiritual side. In order to overcome, it is only through Jesus Christ. And like any athlete will tell you, to overcome, you must be consistent.

Likewise, when it comes to life's trials and tribulations, to be consistent means to continue without changing. Stay the same. Most of us struggle with being consistent in our daily lives. We'll start something with great passion, then quit. If we're not careful, we'll have plenty of things started but never finished, because we fail to be consistent.

It is very important to be consistent in your faith in Christ—believing that He will deliver you from your circumstances. We must remember that **no battle is too hard for God**. He wins every case. With every testimony, there is a test—and with God, you, too, can pass the test.

Whatever you do, don't give up. Claim and speak that you are victorious.

The obstacles that tried to kill me couldn't—because I had Jesus fighting for me. My tests could have kept me down, but because of my foundation, faith, and what Jesus did on the cross, I was lifted every time.

Remember: No matter what Satan throws your way or what life may bring, **Jesus has already overcome your situation.** He overcame when He was beaten, pierced, died, buried, and rose from the grave. When you are on the Lord's side, **you are already victorious**. With that being said, you can shout unto the Lord with the voice of triumph—because you **have the victory**. Always remember: Being victorious doesn't mean I don't have problems. It means I have **peace** while going through my problems.

John 16:33 (KJV): "These things I have spoken unto you, that in me ye might have peace. In the world ye shall have tribulation: but be of good cheer; I have overcome the world."

1 John 5:4–5 (KJV): "For whatsoever is born of God overcometh the world: and this is the victory that overcometh the world, even our faith. Who is he that overcometh the world, but he that believeth that Jesus is the Son of God?"

My prayer is that after reading this book, you will turn to the main source: **Jesus Christ**.

I didn't overcome anything by myself—it was because of Jesus Christ. There's no problem too big that He can't solve. **Jesus is the answer.**

Revelation 12:11 (KJV): "And they overcame him by the blood of the Lamb, and by the word of their testimony."

To God be the glory.

www.ingramcontent.com/pod-product-compliance
Lightning Source LLC
Chambersburg PA
CBHW051247120626
46547CB00014B/1825